THE BASICS OF
WINNING
HORSE-
RACING

Whitney L. Cobb

- Gambling Research Institute -
Cardoza Publishing

CARDOZA PUBLISHING, publisher of **Gambling Research Institute** (GRI) books, is the foremost gaming and gambling publisher in the world with a library of more than 50 up-to-date and easy-to-read books and strategies.

These authoritative works are written by the top experts in their fields and with more than 5,000,000 books in print, represent the best-selling and most popular gaming books anywhere.

PRINTING HISTORY

First Printing	*November 1985*
Second Printing	*September 1987*
Third Printing	*October 1988*

Revised Edition

First Printing	*August 1991*

New Revised Edition

First Printing	*September 1994*
Second Printing	*July 1996*

Copyright © 1985, 1991, 1995 by Gambling Research Institute
- All Rights Reserved -

ISBN:0-940685-49-3
Library of Congress Catalogue Card Number: 94-70606

Cover photo by Michael J. Marten
Charts on pgs. 26, 28-29, 44-45, Copyright ©1994 by Daily Racing Form, Inc.. Reprinted with Permission of the Copyright Owner.
Program on page 7 copyright © Los Angeles Turf Club, Inc.

CARDOZA PUBLISHING
P.O. Box 1500, Cooper Station, New York, NY 10276
Phone (718)743-5229 • Fax (718)743-8284

Table of Contents

I. Introduction   5

II. Understanding the Racing Program   6
The Racing Program

III. The Bets   13
Win, Place and Show Bets • Daily Double • Exacta Betting •
Quinella Betting • Payoffs on Winning Bets

IV. Five Principal Types of Races   19
Stakes Races • Handicap Races • Allowance Races • Maiden
Races • Claiming Races

V. The Daily Racing Form   25
Past Performance Charts • Speed Ratings • Track Variants •
Beyer Speed Figure

VI. Explanation of Abbreviations   38
    Used In Racing Charts
Types of Races • Track Conditions • Finishing Results •
Workouts • Sex of Horses • Color

VII. Understanding the Official   43
    Racing Charts

VIII. Handicapping a Race   49

IX. More Winning Tips   53

Tables and Charts

1. Understanding the Racing Program 7
2. Sample Payoffs: Win, Place and Show 14
3. Payoffs on Winning Bets 17
4. Understanding Past Performance Charts 26
5. Past Performance Charts 28
6. Types of Races 38
7. Track Conditions 40
8. Workout Paces 41
9. Abbreviations Used for Sex of Horse 42
10. Abbreviations Used for Color of Horse 42
11. Official Racing Charts 44

I. Introduction

Welcome to the fascinating world of horse-racing! Going to the track can be an enjoyable experience in itself, but when you're armed with the knowledge necessary to win at the track, it becomes even more pleasurable. And if you can't make it to the track, legitimate casinos often have race books, and there are race books established in Nevada, as well as Off-Track betting offices in New York.

We'll concentrate on all the factors necessary to understand the sport of racing and how to bet on the thoroughbreds. We'll show you how to read a racing program, past performance charts and the official results of races the way the pros read them. We'll also discuss how to handicap horse races, what to look for in the past performance charts to make you a winner, plus a wealth of other information that will help you beat the races.

Betting and winning, that's the name of the game. We'll show you how to do this in our book.

II. Understanding the Racing Program

We'll be dealing with thoroughbred racing on what are known as **flat tracks.** Thoroughbreds can also be trained as steeplechase runners, but here we're concentrating on those who simply run flat races with a jockey on their backs. Standardbreds, a couple of steps lower in the equine hierarchy, race as trotters and pacers with the rider in a sulky (a light, two wheeled carriage), but thoroughbreds have jockeys who ride directly on their backs.

At all racetracks where thoroughbred racing is going on, programs of that day's racing card are sold. Each race gets a separate page in the program, and gives a wealth of information about the race. The study of the program is the first step a bettor takes when wagering money at the track, but in itself, it is not sufficient to give all the information he needs to make an intelligent bet. That will come from the past performance charts as published in the *Daily Racing Form.*

	WIN	PLACE	SHOW	NO.

6 FURLONGS

About 1,200 Meters

6 TH RACE

FRIENDLY HILLS WOMAN'S CLUB

PURSE $21,000. For maidens four years old and upward. Four-year-olds, 117 lbs.; older, 118 lbs.

Track Record—CHINOOK PASS (3) 120 lbs. December 26, 1982 1:07½

MAKE SELECTION BY PROGRAM NUMBER			PROBABLE ODDS
OWNER		TRAINER	JOCKEY

1 Longden & Carr Stables — John Longden
White purple sash, sleeves and cap
BILLIKIN 117
Ch.c.81, Vice Regent—Alibi 4th
10
William Shoemaker

2 Coelho & Valenti — J. R. McCutcheon
Orange, black cap
DAIRYDON 117
Br.c.81, Don B.—Unreachable Star
30
Frank Olivares

3 Summa Stable (Lessee) — George W. Scott
Blue, silver coin on back, silver bar on sleeves, blue and silver cap
COMMANDER'S SONG 117
Ch.c.81, Dust Commander—Char Song
12
Gary Stevens

4 George Putnam — R. W. Mulhall
Red, black and silver sashes and coat-of-arms, red, black and silver cap
BLAME THE DUKE *112
Ch.c.81, Petit Duc—Blame The Apple
15
Dario Lozoya

5 Allen E. Paulson — Gary Jones
White, blue and red emblem, white stars on blue sleeves, red cuffs, blue and red cap
KINETIC 117
B.c.81, Vitriolic—Denim Doll
4
Sandy Hawley

6 Universal Stable — D. Wayne Lukas
Yellow, blue diamond stripes, yellow sleeves, yellow and blue cap
LION OF THE DESERT 117
Ch.c.81, Alydar—Azeez
2
Patrick Valenzuela

7 G. V. D. V. Thoroughbred Farm — John Canty
White, black horseshoe, green "GVDV" on back, white bars and cuffs on green sleeves, green and white cap
SAINT CADVAN 117
Br.c.81, Bold Reason—Mittie Maid
30
Alex Fernandez

8 Roy L. Tyra — James Jordan
Pink, black dots, pink and black cap
COWBOY ROMAN 117
Ch.c.81, Spicey Roman—No More Bells
20
Chris Lamance

9 Elmendorf Farm, Inc. — Gary Jones
Burgundy, gold sash and cap
SUN MASTER 117
B.c.81, Foolish Pleasure—Sunny Today
3
Chris McCarron

10 Wild Plum Farm & Whitham — Mary Lou Tuck
Orange, white blocks on back, white cap
BECAUSE IT'S TRUE 117
Br.c.81, Believe It—Big Rhapsody
6
Terry Lipham

(★) 5 LBS. APPRENTICE ALLOWANCE CLAIMED

EQUIPMENT CHANGE—Lion Of The Desert races without blinkers.

However, without the racing program, the bettor will be in the dark about a number of things that are extremely important to him or her, and in this chapter we'll show just how much one can learn from a racing program.

With this purpose in mind, we're going to examine the program for the 6th Race of January 31, 1985 at Santa Anita Race Track, which is located in Southern California, about thirty miles east of Los Angeles.

Looking at this page, we see the *card* for the 6th race of the day, called the ***Friendly Hills Woman's Club***. Often tracks name races after organizations so that the members of that organization will be well represented at the racetrack that day. It makes for good public relations.

At the very top of the program page we see the term ***Pick Six Race***. This is a gimmick kind of bet in which a bettor must pick the winners of six consecutive races to qualify for an enormous prize. It's very difficult to do, and sometimes days go by without anyone doing it. This has nothing to do with this race, so let's disregard it.

What is important is knowing the distance of the race. This is shown in the diagram in the upper left hand corner; it's a 6 furlong race. **Furlong** is an old English term signifying what was the length of a furrow in farming. But now it's standardized at 220 yards, or 1/8 of a mile. There are 8 furlongs to a mile, and thus, a 6 furlong race is 3/4 of a mile.

Since most thoroughbreds are built and bred for speed, the 6 furlong distance is the most frequently run of all distances, and is the test of the sprinter.

The little black arrow on the top of the diagram shows where the race will begin, and the line across the track of the diagram shows where it will end. A gate is placed where the arrow is located, and all the horses will come out of the gate when they begin their run. They'll finish their race right in front of the grandstand, where the spectators and bettors stay.

Next we discover that the race is for a **purse** of $21,000 and is for maidens. **Maidens** are horses that have never won a race before, and these horses, being four years old and upward, have been running a while without winning a race, since thoroughbreds generally start racing for purses at the age of 2.

All of the four year olds will be assigned a **weight** of 117 pounds; older horses will get 118 pounds. Older horses, being stronger, are penalized slightly for their age.

Then we see the track record for this distance at Santa Anita. It is held by Chinook Pass, who as a three-year-old carrying 120 pounds, ran six furlongs on December 26, 1982 in 1:07-3/5; that is in one minute seven and 3/5 seconds. All fractions of seconds at racetracks are in fifths of seconds, there thus being five fifths to every second when counted as a fraction. The time of 1:07-3/5 is extremely fast, even for a speed track like Santa Anita.

Under this we see "Make Selection By Program Number." At a racetrack, the correct way to bet on a horse is by his program number. If we wanted to bet on the number 1 horse, Billikin, we'd say "$2 to win on number 1," without mentioning the horse's name. When betting at Off-Track Betting parlors in

New York, each horse is assigned a letter instead of a number. At legitimate race books, where there aren't track programs always available, then one might bet using the horse's name.

Now, let's examine the other information available on this program.

Each horse listed has the following information shown next to his name. His owners, his trainer, his jockey, his jockey's colors, his color, the year of his birth, his sire, his dam, the weight the jockey is carrying and the morning line odds. Let's examine these by showing this information on Billikin, the number 1 horse.

Billikin's owners are the Longden & Carr Stables, and his trainer is Johnny Longden, who was one of the legendary jockeys in his day and is now, like many other aging former jockeys, a trainer.

Sometimes knowing the stables that own the horse and the trainer who trains him is important information. Records are kept on the trainer's winning records, and some owners are always trying to win with their horses, while others have lack-luster records. Knowing which trainers are competent, and which owners are trying is information that takes time to find out, but astute bettors make it their business to find out these facts.

Next we come to the colors worn by the jockey. In this case Billikin's jockey will be wearing a white purple sash, sleeves and cap. Track announcers follow the progress of horses around a track during a race by colors rather than numbers oftentimes, and it's easy to follow the horse's progress from the grandstand if you key in on his colors.

The horse's color is stated below his name. Billikin is a chestnut colt (Ch.c) born in 1981, which makes him a four-year-old. His sire was Vice Regent and his dam was Alibi 4th. **Sire** in racing terms means father and **dam** is the mother. For this race he is carrying 117 pounds, and his jockey is William Shoemaker, one of the greatest jockeys who has ever ridden horses. Shoemaker is still riding in his 50s, and holds the record for most wins by a jockey for all time.

The morning line odds on Billikin is 10-1. Morning line odds aren't the actual odds on the horse, but only those suggested by the track linemaker. The actual odds will be determined by the racing and betting public, whose bets will be computed by totalizer (totes or mutuels) and will eventually set the correct odds based on money bet on each horse.

The morning line odds, however, give the racegoer an idea of how the track handicapper sees the chance of each horse in this race. The morning line *favorite* is the number 6 horse, Lion of the Desert, who is 2-1, and the second choice is Sun Master, the number 9 horse.

Astute bettors watch the wagering to see how close the final odds are to the morning line odds. If there's a big discrepancy, they take note of this fact. For example, if a horse is 12-1 on the morning line and is bet down to 3-1, obviously heavy money is coming in from somewhere. And the converse is true. If a horse is 3-1 on the morning line and goes off at 7-1, then insiders know that the horse's condition might not be that great. These aren't infallible methods to spot winners and losers, but they should be weighed, along with other factors.

All the horses in this 6th race are **colts**, that is, male horses under five years of age. They all carry the same weight, 117 pounds, except for Blame the Duke, the number 4 horse, who gets in at 112, because its jockey is an apprentice, and is entitled to a 5 pounds allowance. When Dario Lozoya, the jockey, wins enough races, he loses his *bug* and the mounts he gets won't be entitled to that allowance anymore.

There's also one equipment change in the race. Lion of the Desert will be racing without blinkers. If he's been racing with blinkers steadily, then this change may be meaningful, and after the race, the serious horseplayer should make a note to that effect.

When at a racetrack, be sure to purchase the track's program and to study the information listed. Some of the facts, such as the program number of the horse, is necessary to know in order to bet correctly on that horse. Other information, taken together with the past performance charts, will give the bettor a solid understanding of the horses in the race as well as the conditions relevant to that particular race. Too many bettors disregard the program information, except to find out the number of the horses, but you shouldn't make this mistake.

III. The Bets

In this section, we'll discuss the principal types of wagers that can be made at the track, OTB or a racing book in Nevada.

Win, Place and Show Bets

These are the most popular bets made by the racing public. If a bet is made ($2 minimum) that a horse will **win** the race, that horse must come in first for the bettor to win his or her bet.

If a bet is made for second, or **place**, and the horse finishes in first or second, then the bettor wins his or her wager.

If a bet is made for **show**, or third, and the horse finishes in first, second of third (*in the money*), then the bettor wins.

Payoffs for this type of betting may look like this:

Chart 2
Sample Payoffs: Win, Place and Show

$2 Mutuel Prices:	8 Winning Horse	6.00	3.80	3.20
	6 Second Horse		13.20	5.40
	12 Third Horse			2.80

Only those who have bet the number 8 horse to win would get the $6 payoff. The winning horse went off at 2-1, and the $6 payoff represents $4 at 2-1 and the original $2 bet, for a total of $6. Those who bet for place would get the $3.80 payoff, and those betting show would collect $3.20.

The second horse was a longshot, with a big payoff for place and show, and any bet on this horse for second or third would receive a payoff, but those who bet it to win would lose their bet. The third horse would reward its backers only if they made show bets. For example, if the third horse were bet for win or place, those would be losing bets. Only the show bets, for third, would be paid off.

Daily Double

In order to entice the betting public to attend all the races and arrive early, tracks offer **daily double** betting, which is picking the winner of the first and the second races. A bettor must pick both to get a payoff. Bets on the daily double are at a minimum of $2.

14

The payoff would look like this:

```
$2 Daily Double 4-11 paid $39.20.
```

Since horses at a track are bet on by program number, the number 4 horse won the first race, and the number 11 horse won the second race for this $39.20 payoff.

Exacta Betting

To win an **exacta**, a bettor must pick the horses that finish first and second in the exact order.

At many tracks, only $5 minimum exacta betting is permitted, though at other tracks there are $2.00 exacta bets allowed. The payoff would look like this:

```
$5 Exacta 10-3 paid $215.50.
```

Again, horses are bet by program number rather than by name, and the payoffs reflect this.

Quinella Betting

In **quinella** betting, the player has to pick the first two finishers of the race, but not in correct order, just the winner and place horse. These wagers can be made for as little as $2. A typical payoff would look like this:

```
2 Quinella 8-1 paid $35.60.
```

Sometimes quinella and exacta betting is allowed in the same race. Then a payoff would look like this:

```
$2 Quinella 9-4 paid $39.00 $2 Exacta 4-9 paid $93.40.
```

The exact order of finish was 4 and 9 as reflected by the exacta payoff, which is higher than the quinella payoff because of the level of difficulty in picking the first and second horses finishing in exact order rather than just picking the first two finishers in any order.

There are a number of **gimmick** bets available at different tracks, with very high and exotic payoffs, but the chances of winning these decrease in proportion to the payoffs. Sometimes these are called triples pick six, twin doubles and the most exotic pick nine, in which a player must pick all nine winners to receive the ultimate prize.

We'd suggest that the readers stick to the bets mentioned in this section. Some give good payoffs, and once your handicapping skills are perfected, you can try for other more exotic types of bets.

Payoffs on Winning Bets

It is often difficult for beginners to figure out the correct payoffs for winning bets when the horse they backed comes in first. This is because payoffs are calculated to $2, not $1, and the $2 bet is added to the total. For example, at 3-1, a winning bet would pay off not only the $6 (3-1 x $2) but the original $2 bet as well, for a payoff of $8. The payoff might be a little higher, for the horse might have gone off at 3.20-1 and in this case the payoff would be $8.40. But tote boards at tracks show the odds closest to even numbers, and not those in between. Use the following guide for winning payoffs at a track, the OTB or a race book. All are calculated for $2 bets.

Chart 3
Payoffs on Winning Bets

Odds	Payoff
1-5	$ 2.40
2-5	2.80
3-5	3.20
4-5	3.60
Even (1-1)	4.00
6-5	4.40
7-5	4.80
8-5	5.20
9-5	5.60
2-1	6.00
5-2	7.00
3.1	8.00
7-2	9.00
4-1	10.00
9-2	11.00
5-1	12.00
6-1	14.00
7-1	16.00
8-1	18.00
9-1	20.00
10-1	22.00
15-1	32.00
20-1	42.00
25-1	52.00
30-1	62.00
40-1	82.00
50-1	102.00
60-1	122.00
70-1	142.00
80-1	162.00
90-1	182.00

Usually, tote boards will only go up to 99-1. However, a 99-1 shot on a tote board may very well pay over 100-1.

The higher the odds, the more the likelihood is that the payoff won't be exactly what is shown on this table, but may be higher. For example, a tote board will show odds of 50-1 with the next increment at 55-1 and will not show the exact 54-1 odds that the horse will go off at. In this example, the payoff would be $110 for a $2 ticket instead of $102.

Always remember to add on the original $2 bet when figuring the payout. If you bet more than $2 simply multiply the payoffs by the amount bet, using $2 as the base. For example, if you bet $10 on a 4-1 shot, your payoff would be 5 times the payoff for a $2 bet, or $50.

IV. Five Principal Types of Races

The standard is generally nine races per day at most tracks in the country. Of the nine races per day, most will be claiming races, and there generally will be one feature race which will be either a handicap or a stakes race. The others may be allowance or maiden races. We'll look at each one in order of purse values, with the most lucrative first.

Stakes Races

The top horses are run in **stakes races**, which are the most lucrative of all races, paying the most money to those horses finishing in the money. In these races, the owners of the horses entered put up money, and the racing association or track contributes more money.

For example, the Kentucky Derby, the most famous of all the races run in America, is a stakes race. To enter a horse in this race, the owner must first pay a nominating fee, then other payments up to the time of the running of the race in May of each year.

In addition, the track, Churchill Downs, itself puts up money, which is known as *added* money. This race is the premier race for three-year-olds in America, and is followed by more people with greater interest than any other race. Together with the Preakness and the Belmont Stakes, the Kentucky Derby forms the Triple Crown of racing, the most sought after honor by owners of thoroughbreds. Very few have won the triple crown, but the names of horses like Whirlaway, Count Fleet, Citation, Seattle Slew and Secretariat will always be immortalized because they won the Triple Crown.

There are stakes races for two-year-olds and also for older horses, and some great horses, such as Kelso and John Henry, both **geldings**, that is, male horses that have been unsexed, competed long after other horses were retired to stud, and won fortunes in money for their owners.

Handicap Races

These are the next best money races for horses, and attract top fields of class horses. The weight each horse must carry in the race is assigned separately by the official handicapper at the track so that each of the horses has a chance at winning the race. For example, the horse with the best record, with the most class, gets *top weight* and then other horses, according to their records, get lesser weight. The weakest horse in a handicap event will have the least weight. For example, the top horse may be assigned 126 pounds, while the weakest horse may be assigned ten pounds less.

However, with top horses, added weight is often not sufficient to stop them, and handicapping horses by weight alone is not a sure way to equalize their chances in a particular race. Often, the best horse is given so much weight by a particular handicapper that he is *scratched*, or withdrawn from the race, because of the punishing burden of carrying all that weight.

Horses, especially thoroughbreds, are powerful animals, but they have been bred for certain traits, such as speed, and with too much weight, they are subject to injuries to their legs. Owners of great horses don't want to take the chance of having their horses break down during a race because of added weight on their backs.

Allowance Races

In an **allowance race**, the weights carried by each of the horses are generally set arbitrarily according to the number of races run or amount of money won by each horse entered. For example, in a race for three-year-olds and up (older), the three-year-olds may be assigned a weight of 117 pounds, while all older horses will be assigned 122 pounds.

Allowance races attract horses which aren't of the caliber of stakes or handicap racehorses, but are too valuable to be entered in claiming races, in which the owners may lose their particular horse to another owner.

Since allowance races are run for different amounts of prize money, there are various purses offered for these races. A horse running in an allowance race for a $10,000 purse at a smaller track will be definitely moving up in class if he is entered in an allowance race at a major track for $25,000. And so on, up or down. In the past performance charts, a bettor can see just what kind of race the horse he is thinking of betting on has been used to running. A stakes horse who is entered in an allowance race is definitely going down in class. Often stake horses are entered in allowance races after a long layoff, to give them a race under their belt before attacking the stake races again.

Maiden Races

These are races for valuable horses who haven't yet won a race, and are a cut above claiming races. There is a special category of Maiden Race, called *Maiden Special Weight*, for two-year-old horses who haven't yet won. Often the very best of future stakes winners start their careers in these races, and once they've *broken their maiden*, they move on to stakes races.

Anytime you see a Maiden Race listed, you know the horses entered haven't won a race before, or, if they've won before, it would be a wholly different kind of race, such as a steeplechase, while this race is on a flat dirt or turf (grass) field.

Claiming Races

These are the most frequent kind of races a bettor will encounter at the racetrack. The horses in these races are the bottom of the barrel as far as racing is concerned. The claiming races are the cheapest in terms of purses and horses, of all races at the track.

These cheap races attract basically three different kinds of horses. There are those horses who are moving up in class, and will go from a *claimer* of $5,000 (in which they can be claimed for that sum) to a $6,000 claimer.

Let's explain what is meant by *claiming* at this time. Any horse entered in a claiming race can be claimed or taken away for the claiming price mentioned in the program, by either another owner who has raced horses at that track, or, in unusual cases at some tracks, by anyone who wants to claim the horse.

Other owners who wish to claim a horse must do so prior to the race, not afterwards, in writing. Once a horse is claimed, the new owner runs all the risks of the horse in that race. Should the horse be seriously injured or even have to be destroyed, the claimant is still stuck with that horse.

The purse belongs to the previous owner, however. The official charts of the race will show which horses, if any, have been claimed, and by whom. Usually the claiming owner knows something about the horse; that's why he or she is claiming it. However, often an *also-ran*, a horse finishing out of the money, is claimed.

The second category is a horse moving down in class, going from a $7,500 claimer down to $6,000.

These horses are rapidly going down in class, as their owners desperately try to unload them, since horses are expensive animals to feed and take care of. Or the owner is trying to find a level in which he can win a share of the purse to pay for feed, etc.

The third category is horses of mediocre talent who have no value in stud, and plod along, year after year, racing in claimers, with their owners trying to pick up a few bucks here and there, or unload a horse now and then. Very few horses entered in claimers are claimed by other owners, but the system is very effective in preventing owners from trying to steal a race from weaker horses by entering their horse in a cheap claiming race.

If the horse wins the race, but is claimed, then the owner loses out in the long run, giving up a fine horse just to grab a cheap purse. Claiming races involving cheaper horses, often known as *platers*, make up many of the gimmick races in which daily doubles and triples and exacta betting is allowed. With cheap horses, without consistency and class, it is often difficult to handicap the winner of one of those claiming races.

The cheaper races attract weaker and more inconsistent horses, while the handicap and stakes races attract the best and most consistent horses. Form, as measured by past performance, is more relevant in the better type races.

V. The Daily Racing Form

In order to properly handicap races, the *Racing Form* is a must. At one time it competed with the *Morning Telegraph*, but it's been many years since the *Telegraph* went out of business, and now the *Racing Form* has the field all to itself.

The *Racing Form* covers all the major tracks running in America, so that, with one issue, you can bet or at least handicap races wherever they're run.

The daily newspaper is devoted only to racing, and there's a wealth of information here for the person interested in betting on the ponies. Its main function, however, is showing the past performances of all horses running in all the races.

Only the *Racing Form* has this past performance information, and it is from these past performances that one is able to handicap races.

Each issue contains an explanation of all the information described in a past performance chart. It looks like this:

Past Performance Explanation

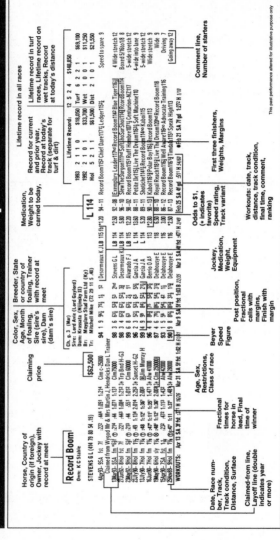

This past performance altered for illustrative purpose only

There is a wealth of information available in the past performance charts. Some handicappers look for only particular factors to study, others look at the whole chart. But whatever a handicapper wants can be found here. It can be said without contradiction that, for the vast majority of horseplayers, the past performance charts are the most important tool they have in figuring out the outcome of a race.

Past Performance Charts

Let's now examine the charts for the horses entered in the 4th race at Santa Anita Park in Arcadia, California for Saturday, March 12, 1994. Before we look at the horse's records, let's first study just what kind of race this is, including the distance to be run.

The race is at a distance of 6 1/2 furlongs, which is a popular sprint distance at Santa Anita, although most sprints at other tracks are run at the more convential 6 furlongs, or 3/4 of a mile. In parentheses, just after the 6 1/2 furlongs is the time 1.14, which is the track record for this distance.

This particular race is an Allowance Race, which means that the horses are better than those entered in Claiming Races, where any horse can be claimed by an owner of racing horses at that meet. However, these ponies are not of the caliber of a Stakes or Handicap Race. The purse is $37,000, which is divided at Santa Anita among the first five horses finishing the race.

The race is for 4-year olds and upward which are non-winners of $3,000 other than maiden or claiming. The weight assigned to each horse is 121 pounds, that is, the

Santa Anita Park

4

6½ Furlongs. **(1:14) ALLOWANCE. Purse $37,000. 4–year–olds and upward which are non–winners of $3,000 other than maiden or claiming. Weight, 121 lbs. Non–winners of a race other than claiming, allowed 3 lbs.**

Meadow Blaze

Own: Centofante J P & Mary

CASTANON A L (90 9 5 5 .10)

Ch. c. 4
Sire: Meadowlake (Hold Your Peace)
Dam: Foolish Miz (Foolish Pleasure)
Br: Lin Drake Farm (Fla)
Tr: Ravin Robert W (—)

121

Lifetime Record :	7 1 1 1	$25,825			
1993	2 1 0 0	$15,950	Turf	0 0 0 0	
1992	5 M 1 1	$9,875	Wet	2 1 1 0	$21,150
SA	5 1 1 1	$25,050	Dist	1 0 1 0	$5,200

22Jan93-6SA gd 1 :231 :48 1:13 1:372 Alw 37000N1X 57 1 5 41½ 66 69½ 721½ Castanon A L B 115 b 20.20 62-17 Personal Hope1155 Union City1184½ Lucky's First One1172½ 7
Rough start, steadied early
9Jan93-6SA my 7f :232 :471 1:12 1:244 Md Sp Wt 77 6 1 11½ 12 11½ 11¾ Castanon A L 118 b 3.90 79-15 Meadow Blaze1181¾ Only Alpha1182 Respectable Rascal1185½ Driving 6
26Dec92-6SA fst 6f :213 :444 :571 1:10 Md Sp Wt 61 5 2 1hd 1hd 74 86½ Castanon A L B 118 b 14.10 80-09 Real Hit1181 Star Of The Eagle1181¾ Nitrogygian1181 Gave way 12
8Nov92-6SA fst 6f :214 :451 :574 1:111 Md Sp Wt 65 7 4 31½ 31½ 33½ 33½ Castanon A L B 118 22.70 76-18 Fort Defiance1183 Sky Gypsy118½ Meadow Blaze118 Always close 11
31Oct92-12SA my 6½f :214 :452 1:113 1:182 Md Sp Wt 64 4 1 31½ 32½ 32 23½ Castanon A L B 117 19.00 74-18 Cut ToRun1173½ MeadowBlaze117 ShadowLauncher117 4-wide stretch 6
22Aug92-6Dmr fst 6f :214 :45 :57 1:09 Md Sp Wt 39 3 7 43 77¾ 510 523½ Pincay L Jr B 117 45.10 70-05 Seattle Sleet117½ River Special1178 Chayim117 Stopped 8
29Jly92-6Dmr fst 5½f :212 :45 1:034 Md Sp Wt 45 6 10 1011 108¾ 109½ 712½ Pincay L Jr B 117 22.50 79-07 Devil Diamond1176 Dare To Duel117½ Sudden Hush117 Off poorly, wide 10

WORKOUTS: ●Mar 9 Hol 3f fst :343 H *1/17* ●Mar 2 Hol 6f fst 1:123 H *1/11* Feb 23 Hol 6f fst 1:141 H *4/8* Feb 16 Hol 6f fst 1:17 H *22/23* Feb 11 Hol 5f fst 1:024 H *33/41* Feb 2 Hol 4f fst :493 H *11/17*

Dry Gulch

Own: Connell James A

GONZALEZ S JR (258 31 22 34 .12)

B. c. 4
Sire: Gulch (Mr. Prospector)
Dam: Funny Tammy (Tentam)
Br: Paliafito James L & Roissard Leo Gatto (Ky)
Tr: Trevino Stephen G (5 1 0 0 .20)

L 116⁵

Lifetime Record :	10 1 2 0	$23,600			
1994	2 0 0 0		Turf	1 0 0 0	
1993	7 1 2 0	$23,600	Wet	0 0 0 0	
SA	5 0 1 0	$8,925	Dist	1 0 0 0	$2,175

27Jan94-7SA fst 1 :22 :452 1:101 1:353 Alw 40000N1X 66 8 3 33½ 41¼ 68½ 713¼ Nakatani C S LB 120 b 19.00 78-16 Tossofthecoin1201¼ Barton1171¼ Outside The Line120½ Wide into lane 9
19Jan94-6SA fst 6f :214 :444 :564 1:091 Alw 37000N1X 75 11 6 73¾ 74½ 107¼ 107 Nakatani C S LB 120 b 22.80 84-11 Ke Express117hd Whosthepurplecomet117no Mistive1172½ No rally 11
18Dec93-4Hol fst 1⅟₁₆ ⊗ :224 :46 1:111 1:444 3↑ Md Sp Wt 73 8 4 31½ 3nk 11½ 12¾ Nakatani C S LB 118 b 4.10 77-14 DH Regal Rowdy121 DH Dry Gulch1182¾ Bavar1184½ 5 wide 1st turn 9
27Nov93-2Hol fst 7f :222 :452 1:103 1:233 3↑ Md 50000 71 1 3 22 22 21 2½ Flores D R LB 119 b *1.90 85-11 Boron119½ Dry Gulch1193½ Greenspan1191¾ Inside bid 7
23Oct93-6SA fst 1 :222 :454 1:11 1:363 3↑ Md Sp Wt 71 2 2 2hd 2hd 41½ 512 Flores D R LB 117 b 6.10 75-10 Vegieman1173½ Sky Gypsy1171 Remarfable1121 Dueled between 7
6Sep93-5Dmr fm 1⅟₁₆ Ⓣ :234 :48 1:124 1:431 3↑ Md Sp Wt 53 10 4 52¼ 53½ 710 715 Delahoussaye E LB 118 4.40 75-10 CherokeeTribute113½ Gian'sBigBrek1182¼ Recommendtion118½ Faltered 10
15Aug93-4Dmr fst 6f :22 :444 :571 1:10 3↑ Md Sp Wt 73 7 11 1110 1111 88¾ 66 Delahoussaye E LB 117 5.50 83-11 Spartan Order117nk Ballet Aly1173½ Turbie1171 Rough start, wide 12
14Feb93-6SA fst 1⅟₁₆ :231 :464 1:113 1:443 Md Sp Wt 78 4 3 21½ 32 3½ 2hd Desormeaux K J B 117 *2.30 81-16 Big Way117hd Dry Gulch1171¾ Mc Comas1175 11
Head struck by foe's whip 1/16
24Jan93-6SA fst 6½f :22 :451 1:103 1:172 Md Sp Wt 69 6 10 108¾ 88½ 65½ 42¾ Valenzuela P A B 118 10.60 81-15 Zignew118¾ Niner Bush1181¾ T. H. Fappiano118nk Poor start 10
19Dec92-4Hol fst 6f :221 :451 :573 1:102 Md Sp Wt 64 3 7 75¼ 76¾ 66 66 Nakatani C S 118 10.20 82-10 Personal Hope1183¼ Ballet Aly118nk Duane118no Off slowly, wide 8

Own: Blanchard Dr Lucius
Dam: Maharanee Rose (Raja Baba)
Br: Blanchard Lucius (Ky)
Tr: Rash Rodney (68 6 8 12 .09)
ANTLEY C W (255 35 27 15 .14)
L 121

1994	1 0 0 0	$925	Turf	2 0 0 1	$6,300
1993	5 0 1 1	$17,500	Wet	0 0 0 0	
SA	4 1 1 0	$24,175	Dist	3 0 1 0	$9,575

2Feb94-6SA fst 6½f :22 :45 1:091 1:153 Alw 37000N1X 85 4 6 86 84 64½ 53¾ Stevens G L LB 120 9.60 90-13 Classic Advance117¾ Demigod120no Lil Orphan Moonie1181 Late interest 8
8Dec93-8Hol fst 6½f :214 :442 1:082 1:14 3↑ Alw 30000N1X 80 4 5 43 22½ 45 410½ Black C A LB 119 2.60 88-08 Pharaoh's Heart1165½ Classic Advance1162½ Polar Route1112½ Weakened 7
3Nov93-3SA fst 6½f :221 :444 1:093 1:161 3↑ Alw 32000N1X 89 3 6 64½ 43½ 21½ 2nk Black C A LB 118 2.70 90-14 Spartan Order118nk Nevada Range1182 Private Isle1161¼ Late foot 6
8Oct93-7SA fst 1 :23 :47 1:11 1:354 Alw 34000N1X 90 1 6 52½ 42½ 42¾ 44¾ Black C A LB 117 3.80 86-17 Dinand1203 I'm Checkin' Out1171¼ Wild Bamboo117½ Mild late bid 8
10Sep93-7Dmr fm 1 1/16 Ⓣ :243 :494 1:141 1:442 3↑ Alw 36000N2L 80 4 3 31 31 42 52 Black C A LB 115 3.00 82-10 CrackerjaxMx115¾ SwissMirge122no DelMrDennis110no Boxed in 3/8-3/16 7
22Aug93-5Dmr fm 1 1/16 Ⓣ :25 :503 1:152 1:444 Alw 36000N1X 83 5 4 41½ 51½ 31½ 32¼ Black C A LB 117 5.40 80-09 Whata Boom117no Minjinsky1172¼ Nevada Range117no Always close 10
14Nov92-8BM fst 1 :23 :47 1:113 1:371 L Stanford54k 81 7 7 78½ 53¾ 42½ 32¼↓ Boulanger G 114 5.30 82-20 Yappy116nk Lykatill Hil1182 DH Gary Go Go114 Rallied inside 8
Dead heat
11Oct92-2SA fst 6f :214 :444 :572 1:102 Md Sp Wt 84 4 5 76¾ 46 23 11¾ Solis A B 117 7.00 84-16 Nevada Range1171¾ Fact Book1172¼ Fort Defiance117 Inside rally 8
WORKOUTS: Mar 9 SA 3f fst :37 B 3/20 Feb 28 SA 7f fst 1:284 H 7/7 Feb 22 SA 6f fst 1:152 H 37/44 Feb 13 SA 3f fst :36 H 5/24 Jan 30 SA 3f fst :394 H 39/40 Jan 22 SA 7f fst 1:262 H 7/12

Snoboy

Own: Burke Gary W & Timothy R
Dk. b or br g. 7
Sire: Gumboy (Gummo)
Dam: Winter Favorite (Bold Favorite)
Br: Roberts Mr & Mrs G C (Wash)
Tr: Mitchell Mike (71 12 14 12 .17)
STEVENS G L (293 41 63 52 .14)
L 118

Lifetime Record : 59 9 16 8 $97,800

1994	4 2 1 0	$18,225	Turf	0 0 0 0	
1993	13 1 4 1	$11,005	Wet	3 1 1 1	$7,105
SA	5 2 1 0	$18,550	Dist	15 2 3 4	$28,369

26Feb94-7SA fst 6f :22 :443 :563 1:091 Alw 37000N1X 88 1 4 64½ 64 65¾ 52½ Nakatani C S LB 118 fb 2.90 88-11 Whosthepurplecomet117¾ Forest Joy117½ Demigod120hd Mild late bid 7
3Feb94-5SA fst 6f :213 :444 :563 1:084 Clm 16000 101 6 1 75½ 51¾ 13 14 Nakatani C S LB 117 b 3.00 93-09 Snoboy1174 To Be A Saros1121 Five Sharps117¾ Circled field, best 11
20Jan94-7SA fst 6½f :22 :443 1:084 1:151 Clm 16000 94 4 2 62¾ 43 3½ 2½ Nakatani C S LB 116 b 5.60 95-08 No Commitment116½ Snoboy1161¾ I'm Huge116¾ Inside bid 11
5Jan94-1SA fst 6f :212 :442 :57 1:092 Clm c-10000 84 5 10 98¼ 96¾ 1½ 13 Antley C W LB 116 b 3.70 90-09 Snoboy1163 Tu Eres Mi Heroe116¾ Mistery Kid1161¼ Wide trip 11
Claimed from Taylor John, Penney Jim Trainer
26Dec93-1SA fst 6f :213 :441 :563 1:091 3↑ Clm 12500 87 3 7 63¼ 41¾ 52 53 Valenzuela P A LB 117 b 25.20 88-09 Burn And Turn1171 Ocean Native111½ I'm Huge1161½ Outfinished 9
28Nov93-6YM fst 5½f :232 :463 :594 1:063 3↑ Clm 10000 70 1 6 25 22 2½ 2no D'Amico D L LB 119 b 3.40 80-19 Impco119no Snoboy1192 York's Special1191½ Just missed 7
19Oct93-7EP fst 6½f :222 :452 1:102 1:164 3↑ Clm 11500 85 3 1 43 42¾ 31½ 1hd Cooper B L 120 fb 7.65 96-11 Snoboy120hd Flashing Pass1192 Martini To Tango116hd Just up 6
6Oct93-7EP fst 6½f :223 :454 1:103 1:171 3↑ Clm 11500 77 2 1 44 32 31½ 31¾ Cooper B L 120 fb 38.30 92-18 Lasting Obsidian1191 Flashing Pass119¾ Snoboy1202¼ Closed evenly 7
20Sep93-5YM fst 6f :223 :45 :571 1:092 Clm 10000 60 8 5 77 66 69½ 56 Cooper B LB 120 fb 12.70 90-09 Going To Maui1171½ Abergwaun Pistol1172 Kelp116no No threat 9
2Sep93-10YM fst 6f :224 :452 :574 1:101 Clm 10000 52 7 7 77¾ 76½ 67¾ 87½ Aragon V A LB 116 fb *2.70 84-14 Pete N Repete1221 Mickey Le Scott122½ Premium Gallo1201½ Outrun 9
WORKOUTS: Mar 7 Hol 4f fst :494 H 15/22 Feb 19 Hol 4f fst :484 H 18/24 Feb 14 Hol 3f fst :362 H 2/5 Jan 29 Hol 3f fst :363 H 8/19 Jan 1 SA 5f fst 1:013 H 32/42 Dec 24 SA 3f fst :353 H 4/39

Boron

Own: Risdon A G & L G
B. g. 4
Sire: Classic Go Go (Pago Pago)
Dam: Ellis Island (First Landing)
Br: Verne H. Winchell (Ky)
Tr: Risdon Larry G (4 1 1 0 .25)
VALENZUELA P A (195 21 18 35 .11)
118

Lifetime Record : 2 1 0 0 $10,450

1994	1 0 0 0		Turf	0 0 0 0	
1993	1 1 0 0	$10,450	Wet	0 0 0 0	
SA	1 0 0 0		Dist	0 0 0 0	

5Feb94-5SA fst 1 :222 :454 1:102 1:362 Clm c-40000 55 5 1 2hd 67 920 921¾ Almeida G F B 115 20.50 65-12 MistingRain1174½ WelcomeDay115½ DaneboStampede115½ Used up early 9
Claimed from V H W Stables, McAnally Ronald Trainer
27Nov93-2Hol fst 7f :222 :452 1:103 1:233 3↑ Md 50000 72 2 4 12 12 11 1½ Almeida G F B 119 2.00 86-11 Boron119½ Dry Gulch1193½ Greenspan1191¾ Gamely 7
WORKOUTS: Mar 9 SA 4f fst :472 H 4/57 Mar 1 SA 6f fst 1:14 H 8/16 Feb 22 SA 4f fst :481 H 30/88 Jan 31 Hol 6f fst 1:134 H 4/11 Jan 25 Hol 6f fst 1:134 H 6/11 ●Jan 13 Hol 7f fst 1:262 H 1/8

weight the jockey carries. Non-winners of a race other than claiming, allowed 3 pounds. That's why several horses will have different weights assigned. Meadow Blaze and Nevada Range will carry the full weight of 121 pounds.

However, Boron, Snoboy, Cheesebiscuit and El Travieso (the latter two not shown), will carry a weight of 118 pounds, which means that they are non-winners of a race other than a claiming race. And finally, Dry Gulch will carry 116 pounds. The small 5 next to 116 means that there will be an apprentice jockey on the horse, with a 5 pound apprentice allowance.

Note that next to the weight on several horses there is a "L". This means that the horse has the medication known as *Lasix*, which is an anti-bleeding medication. Thus we see not only the weight of the horse, but the medication the horse is on that day. Lasix, though legal in California, is not legal in several other states.

The two most important things that the past performance charts don't show are the name of the jockey riding the horse and the morning line odds. This information will have to come from the program at the track, or, if betting at a casino or legitimate sports book, they'll have this information posted prior to post time.

Not only does the bettor find out about the past performances of each horse, but there is information about his color, as well as his breeding. There is also information about the owner and trainer of the horse. Some stables are followed closely because they have their horses sharp and fit, with good trainers.

Let's look at Meadow Blaze. He is a charcoal colt,

four years old. After the age of 4, he would be refereed to as a horse. The same with fillies. At the age of 5 they're referred to as mares.

His sire is Meadowlake, and Meadowlake's sire was Hold Your Peace. Meadow Blaze's dam was Foolish Miz, and her sire was Foolish Pleasure. This information can be important, because breeding plays a big role in horse racing, and some horses are bred for speed and some for stamina.

Meadow Blaze is a sprinter, and has not run, as far as the past performance chart shows, in a race over 7 furlongs, which is a longish sprint, except for his last start about two months before, at Santa Anita. In that race, he ran for a mile and was badly beaten. His trainers after that race have once more entered him in a sprint.

For a four year old, he has been lightly race, with only eight races under his belt. We see that his lifetime record is 7 starts, with one first, place and show finish, and a total purse win of $25,825.

Meadow Blaze's one win was at Santa Anita, on a muddy track, where he won leading wire to wire, in a 7 furlong race. He also place second in another muddy race, which might account for him going off at only 3.90-1 in his winning effort. In that winning race, his **speed rating** was 79-15, which means that compared to the track record, which would be 100, he ran a 79, rather a mediocre time. Since it was a muddy track, we look at the other number, the 16 **variant** which means that the average horse running that day was 16 points off the 100 rating, for an average of 84. Meadow Blaze was below that average, with only a 79.

In addition to the speed rating, the charts now show the **Beyer Speed Figure**, devised by Andrew Beyer. This is a comparative figure, and can be used to rate various horses in a race.

For example, Nevada Range has a Beyer Speed Figure of from 80 to 90 in his races, while Meadow Blaze's highest Beyer Speed Figure was only 77, in the one race he won. Obviously, according to this Speed Figure, Nevada Range is a much better horse than Meadow Blaze.

Getting back to the track variant. It can mean either the quality of the horses running that day, the condition of the track, or both. Speed ratings are important when a group of horses have run at the same track. The quality of horses at a major track such as Belmont or Santa Anita will be better than those at a lesser-known track, and a horse with a 95 speed rating at Golden Gate Fields wouldn't compare favorably with a 90 rating at Santa Anita. Similarly, a 95 rating at Woodbine wouldn't match a 90 rating at Belmont.

Thus, speed ratings must be examined in perspective. They will have validity only when at comparable tracks. In New York, for example, the speed ratings, at Belmont, Aqueduct and Saratoga will be fairly comparable. All are punishing tracks with deep soil, not the cardboard fast tracks favored in the West. Plus the caliber of the horses running at these tracks is very high. They're the best.

A further examination of Meadow Blaze's races reveal that he kept running in Maiden Special Weight races rather than Claiming Races, and after five winless races, he **broke his maiden** in his sixth race.

He has some good breeding, and the owners don't want to put him in a Claiming Race, where he might be claimed away, so they are running him in Allowance Races now.

In this same race today is a 7 year old gelding named Snoboy. He has run in 59 races, considerably more than any of the other horses. Geldings, which of course cannot be bred, are usually run more often than horses or colts.

Snoboy has been having a fine time in the speed rating department, with many of his races showing over 90. He has won a 6 furlong race in the excellent time of $1:08^{x24}$, or one minute eight and four-fifths seconds, earning him a speed rating of 93, and Beyer Figure of 101. He has also won three out of the last seven races he's been entered in, and is sharp, according to the charts. Even in his last race, Snoboy finished sixth, but only 2 1/2 lengths out of first place. In the morning line, he'll go off at much shorter odds than Meadow Blaze.

A gelding like Snoboy has been castrated. There are various reasons why this is done, from poor breeding prospects to taming an unruly horse. Male horses are occasionally gelded as the only way to control and train them correctly for running. Some of the greatest horses in the history of American racing, such as Kelso and John Henry, have been geldings. Indeed, the greatest money winner of all time was John Henry, and Kelso wasn't far behind.

Geldings of high quality often win enormous sums of money for their owners because they're allowed to race into their 9th and 10th years, since they can't be retired for stud purposes. On the other hand, many great horses are retired early, often in the third or fourth years, for they become much more valuable to the owners as stud horses, commanding enormous fees for breeding purposes.

Thus we see Snoboy, a gelding, as the oldest horse in the race, still making money for his owners. In addition to his overall winnings, he has also made the most money in 1994 among the horses entered in this race.

Another interesting entry is Boron. Although a four year old, and a gelding, he has only raced twice in his lifetime, once in November, 1993 and again in February, 1994. He went off in his initial start at 2-1, and won gamely, taking the lead and holding on. However, his next race at 1 mile (previously he had run at 7 furlongs) was a disaster. Going off at 20.50-1, he was used up early and finished 9th by almost 22 lengths. He was claimed in that race, and is now running for a new owner.

Top horses have consistency. Those below the top, even in Allowance Races, run hot and cold, and though they may win one day, they can be far behind the next time out. This is seen time and time again. Look at Dry Gulch. After breaking his maiden, he was moved up in class to Allowance Races where he finished tenth and seventh respectively.

In this section, we're not handicapping the race, just showing the number of factors that can be considered from reading the past performance charts. They tell us all we have to know about the past ten races each horse has run (if he's had that many races under his belt) but the race we have to bet on will reveal the present condition of each horse.

However, by that time we've made our bets and it's too late to change our minds. So, we turn to another bit of information shown in these charts that may help us understand the horse's present condition, and that is the workout times. These are listed at the bottom of each horse's charts.

These are important only if they've taken place *after* the last posted race. Meadow Blaze has been working out at Hollywood Park, also in the Lows Angeles area, and he has done six furlongs, **handily,** in his best workout at 1:12^3. Handily, or i**n hand**,is faster than **breezing**. Nevada Range's last workout at Santa Anita was breezing, 3 furlongs in :37. It is clear, looking at the workouts, that most of these horses have been given hard rides in their tuneups for the race today.

Study the charts, including the comment line at the end of each race, to get the best possible picture of the race you're going to bet on. It is all the variables we've been discussing in this chapter that makes handicapping so fascinating and difficult at the same time. Everything is in front of us; and yet the horse that seems best doesn't always win the race. Nor does the horse that goes off s the favorite; it only wins about one-third of the time.

Incidentally, on a clear and fast track, Snoboy, going off as the favorite at 1.70-1, won the race by 1 1/4 lengths, over Cheesebiscuit (not shown), the third choice at 3.10-1. Meadow Blaze finished third, going off at

26.60-1. Nevada Range, the second betting choice at 2.80-1, finished sixth by 36 lengths. Boron lost his rider and did not finish.

Speed Ratings

A speed rating compares the horse's final time to the track record at that distance established in prior season. This track record has a rating of 100. Since a difference of length (horse's length) is approximately 1/5 of a second, for each 1/5 of a second that the horse is slower than the track record, one point is deducted.

Thus, if a horse is two seconds off the track record (10 lengths behind) he would receive a speed rating of 90. Should a horse be 10 lengths behind the winning horse in a race, in which the winner was one second slower than the track record, then that losing horse's speed rating would only be 85. For example, if the track record for 6 furlongs was 1:09, and the winner ran the race in 1:10, then the horse 10 lengths behind would have a time of approximately 1:12 and the 85 speed rating.

Track Variant

Next to the speed rating is another number, called the **track variant.** For example, if the speed rating is 85 for a horse, you might see 85-18. The second number, 18, is the track variant.

This is calculated by taking into consideration the distance of a race, short or long. The track variant is the average number of points (or lengths) either faster or slower than the three-year best time record for all horses running on the same program the same day the same conditions (short or long, dirt or grass).

Under the formula, separate track variants are computed for races under one mile (short) and at one mile and over (long) both on dirt and grass. Within these categories, separate variants are also calculated if there is a change in track condition during the course of the program (from fast to sloppy or muddy on the dirt; from firm to soft or yielding on the grass).

For example, if the average speed rating came to 82 for winning horses in the sprints (under one mile) while the track was fast, then that number is subtracted from 100, giving us a track variant for that day of 18, the difference between 100 and 82. The lower the track variant, the faster the track that day, or the quality of the horses running was better.

Beyer Speed Figure

This figure, devised by Andrew Beyer, has been incorporated into the past performance charts since 1992, and is another method of grading the horse's performance in a particular race on a particular day.

Beyer takes into consideration the surface, the class of horses, the distances and the average times run on the day of the race, and makes a summary of the day's card. He also uses a number of other adjustments, which are not revealed, and comes up with a Speed Figure.

Many race bettors depend on this figure in evaluating a horse's performance, and have more confidence in it rather than the speed rating and track variant, also available on the charts.

VI. Explanation of Abreviations Used in Racing Charts

There are a number of abbreviations that should be known by horseplayers in order to better understand the information presented in racing charts. The following are the ones most frequently encountered.

Types of Race.

The *Daily Racing Form* designates a claiming race simply by showing a money amount without any other notation.

Chart 6
Types of Races

15000—This would indicate a claiming race in which this horse could be claimed for $15,000. If the horse had been claimed in that race, the notation would read: **c15000**.

M15000—Maiden Claiming Race.

15000H—Claiming Handicap Race.

Other race categories are as follows:

Mdn—Maiden Race, in which none of the horses have won a race previously.

AlwM—Maiden Allowance Race for non-winners with special weight allowances.

Aw36000—An Allowance Race, showing the purse value of the race.

Hcp—Handicap Race. When the reading is **HcpO**, it means an overnight handicap race.

Stakes Races—In a Stakes Race, the name of the race is listed, or an abbreviation of that name. When you see just a name listed, such as Preakness or Gold Cup, you know that this is a stakes race. When there's an H next to the stakes name, such as Bing CrosbyH at Del Mar, then it's a stakes handicap race.

Track Conditions

In the past performance charts, the condition of the track is listed next to the time of the race. For example, if the final time in a 6 furlong race is listed as 1:11²ft, then we know the track was fast for that time. If it had been listed as 1:11²gd, the time for that race was run by a horse on a good track.

It's important to know the symbols for track conditions because some horses prefer mud and slop and others will only do their best on a fast track. If a horse has an off race it may be due solely to track conditions.

Chart 7
Track Conditions

Ft—Fast track. The track is dry and hard.

Gd—Good track. The track is not quite dry.

Sl—Slow track. The track is wet and drying out, but not good.

Sly—Sloppy track. The track is firm with puddles of water on its surface.

My—Muddy track. The track is soft from top to bottom.

Hy—Heavy track. The track features the slowest of all conditions.

Finishing Results

The order of the horse's finish is signified by a number. If the horse came in first, it would be a 1. After the number is the winning margin. The narrowest of margins is a nose, then comes a head, then a neck. These are listed as follows in the past performance and official racing charts:

no—nose
hd—head
nk—neck

The following would show a horse's running of a race, with position and margins. If a horse is not in the lead, then the number after his position would indicate how many lengths he's behind the leader.

6^3 $4^{2\frac{1}{2}}$ 3^{nk} 2^{hd} 1no $1^{1\frac{1}{2}}$

The horse was first sixth, three lengths behind the leader, then he improved his position to fourth, 2½ lengths behind the first horse, then he was third by a neck, then second by a head, then took the lead by a nose, then won the race by 1½ lengths.

Workouts

In order for bettors to get a better indication of the condition of a horse, especially one that hasn't raced for a while, he or she can examine the workouts of the horse. These are listed under the past performances for each horse, showing the date, the time of the workout, and how the horse was handled.

Let's look at a sample workout to see what all this means.

Aug 23 Sar 5f gd 1:01 h

The horse had a workout on August 23rd at Saratoga, the distance was 5 furlongs on a good track, and the time was one minute and one second, and the horse ran handily.

In workouts, horses aren't usually pushed to the limit the way they are in a race, and so the workout times are generally much slower than the actual time the horse could run the race. Also horses don't usually break from a gate, and simply run from one furlong pole to another, and are timed for that distance. The following are abbreviations commonly used in workouts:

Chart 8
Workout Paces

b—breezing	
e—easily	**d—driving**
h—handily	**g—worked from gate**

Workout times are often deceptive because the horses aren't working from a gate and aren't in competition with other horses and are not running at full speed, but sometimes it's a good indication of the condition of the horse, especially if you see the letter "d" indicating that the horse was driving, going all out.

Sex of Horse

There are six categories listed under sex.

Chart 9
Abbreviations Used for Sex of Horse

c—**Colt.** This is a male horse under the age of 5 years.

f—**Filly.** This is a female under the age of 5 years.

h—**Horse.** This is a male 5 years or older.

m—**Mare.** This is a female five years or older.

g—**Gelding.** This is an unsexed or gelded male of any age.

rig—Ridgling. This is a horse with undescended testicles (half-castrated) of any age.

Color

Horses come in a variety of colors, ranging from black to white, with browns predominating.

Chart 10
Abbreviations Used for Color of Horse

Ch—Chestnut	B—Bay.
Gr—Gray	Blk—Black.
Ro—Roan	Br—Brown
Wh—White	

Dk—Dark, as in Dk b or Dk br, which would mean dark bay or dark brown.

VII. Understanding the Official Racing Charts

The Official Racing Charts show the results of each race run, so that not only do we know the order of finish of all the horses, but observations are made about each horse's results. The serious bettor would do well to save these charts and examine them. They, together with the past performance charts, give a very clear picture of just how each horse did in a particular race.

Let's examine several of the official racing charts for Wednesday, March 9, 1994 at Santa Anita Race Track in Arcadia, California.

Santa Anita is set in picturesque country, with a backdrop of the San Gabriel Mountains. The building is set in Art Deco and the grounds are spacious and comfortable, with ample parking facilities. There is both a dirt and turf track, with most races run on dirt.

The first race was on dirt at 6 1/2 furlongs. Eight

FIRST RACE Santa Anita MARCH 9, 1994

6½ FURLONGS. (1.14) CLAIMING. Purse $11,000. 4-year-olds and upward. Weight 121 lbs. Non-winners of two races since February 1, allowed 3 lbs. Of a race since February 15, 5 lbs. Claiming price $10,000. (Maiden or races when entered for $8,500 or less not considered.)(Day 55 of a 90 Day Meet. Clear. 70.)

Value of Race: $11,000 Winner $6,050; second $2,200; third $1,650; fourth $825; fifth $275. Mutuel Pool $209,165.00 Exacta Pool $162,902.00 Quinella Pool $31,208.00

Last Raced	Horse	M/Eqt.	A.	Wt	PP	St	¼	½	Str	Fin	Jockey	Cl'g Pr	Odds $1
3Feb94 5SA11	Diable Rouge	LB	6	116	5	1	2 1½	2 2	2 3½	1 nk	Castanon A L	10000	1.20
24Feb94 5SA2	Friedlander	LB	6	116	2	2	1 1	1 1½	1 ½	2 2¼	Pedroza M A	10000	3.30
24Feb94 5SA1	Marlar	LBbf	7	118	6	3	3 ½	3 1½	3 hd	3 3	Solis A	10000	2.40
24Feb94 5SA6	Value The Venue	LB	4	117	3	4	4 1	4 1	4 2	4 2¾	Sorenson D	10000	8.30
16Feb94 5SA5	Baba Ran	LBf	7	116	1	5	5 1½	6	5 hd	5 ¾	Valenzuela F H	10000	15.40
2Mar94 5SA6	Mickey Le Scott	LBbf	6	116	4	6	6	5 hd	6	6	Antley C W	10000	22.20

OFF AT 12:31 Start Good. Won driving. Time, :22 3, :46, 1:10, 1:16 2 Track fast.

$2 Mutuel Prices:

6-DIABLE ROUGE	4.40	3.80	2.20
3-FRIEDLANDER		3.80	2.20
8-MARLAR			2.10

$2 EXACTA 6-3 PAID $15.60 $2 QUINELLA 3-6 PAID $10.20

B. h, by Mamaison-Crimson Cameo, by Crimson Satan. Trainer Shulman Sanford. Bred by Horn E & Lillyan (Ky).

DIABLE ROUGE jumped a shadow leaving the chute, prompted the pace outside FRIEDLANDER to the stretch and just edged that rival despite jumping the mirror reflection at the wire. FRIEDLANDER was hustled to the early lead off the rail, set the pace off the fence and finished gamely but could not quite hold off the winner. MARLAR raced off the rail throughout and held the show. VALUE THE VENUE outside BABA RAN early, saved ground thereafter but lacked a rally. BABA RAN was taken a bit off the rail on the backstretch and also failed to rally. MICKEY LE SCOTT off awkwardly, raced wide and was outrun. MUSTANG MARVEL (1) REPORTED SICK, AND MINT JUBILEE (7) AND BERING GIFTS (9) BOTH REPORTED INJURED, WERE SCRATCHED BY THE STEWARDS ON THE ADVICE OF THE TRACK VETERINARIAN. ALL REGULAR, EXACTA, QUINELLA AND DOUBLE WAGERS ON THEM WERE ORDERED REFUNDED AND ALL THEIR PLACE PICK NINE SELECTIONS WERE SWITCHED TO THE FAVORITE, DIABLE ROUGE (6).

Owners— 1, Scarlett Roger J; 2, Carava & Osterberg & Travato; 3, Marcus Martin L; 4, Kirkwood Al & Sandee; 5, Reynoso & Sierra; 6, Sherman Ernest D

Trainers—1, Shulman Sanford; 2, Carava Jack; 3, Young Steven W; 4, Puhich Michael; 5, Payan Ruben; 6, Penney Jim

Overweight: Value The Venue (1).

Diable Rouge was claimed by Bowman David; trainer, Chambers Mike.,

Friedlander was claimed by Koriner & Shannon; trainer, Koriner Brian.

Scratched— Mustang Marvel (11Feb94 5SA3), Mint Jubilee (19Jan94 6SA11), Be One Bomber (4Feb94 6GG7), Bering Gifts (16Feb94 1SA8)

SECOND RACE Santa Anita MARCH 9, 1994

1 1/16 MILES. (1.39) CLAIMING. Purse $20,000. Fillies and mares, 4-year-olds and upward. Weight, 121 lbs. Non-winners of two races at one mile or over since February 1, allowed 3 lbs. Of such a race since February 15, 5 lbs. Claiming price $20,000; if for $18,000, 2 lbs. (Maiden or races when entered for $16,000 or less not considered.)

Value of Race: $20,000 Winner $11,000; second $4,000; third $3,000; fourth $1,500; fifth $500. Mutuel Pool $302,401.00 Exacta Pool $257,495.00 Quinella Pool $48,203.00

Last Raced	Horse	M/Eqt.	A.	Wt	PP	St	¼	½	¾	Str	Fin	Jockey	Cl'g Pr	Odds $1
23Feb94 7SA5	Gordy's Dancer	LB	4	115	6	4	2 hd	2 hd	2 1½	1 2	1 1¼	Nakatani C S	18000	10.60
4Mar94 7SA4	Moms Baby	LB	5	116	4	7	5 ½	4 1½	3 hd	3 2	2 2½	Stevens G L	20000	3.50
27Jan94 3SA4	Charisma	LBb	6	116	1	3	7 1½	7 hd	7 1½	4 1	3 ½	Solis A	20000	4.00
11Feb94 1SA3	Oh Sweet Thing	LB	7	116	2	1	4 1	5 hd	6 hd	5 2	4 ½	Flores D R	20000	3.00
17Feb94 6GG5	Magic Moon-Br	LBf	6	116	3	2	1 1½	1 1	1 ½	2 ½	5 2	Gryder A T	20000	8.50
23Feb94 7SA3	Madame Bovary	LBb	6	111	8	8	8	8	8	6 2½	6 8½	Gonzalez S Jr5	20000	5.10
25Feb94 2SA1	Fager's Prospect	LBb	4	116	5	6	6 1½	6 1	5 hd	8	7 2¼	Desormeaux K J	20000	11.10
23Feb94 7SA1	Northern Wool	LBb	4	116	7	5	3 1½	3 1	4 2	7 ½	8	Valenzuela F H	20000	11.30

OFF AT 1:00 Start Good. Won driving. Time, :23 2, :47 2, 1:12, 1:37 1, 1:43 4 Track fast.

$2 Mutuel Prices:

6-GORDY'S DANCER	23.20	9.80	6.00
4-MOMS BABY		4.80	3.20
1-CHARISMA			3.40

$2 EXACTA 6-4 PAID $119.00 $2 QUINELLA 4-6 $53.60

B. f, by Northern Baby-Tangled Love, by Sir Ivor. Trainer Stein Roger M. Bred by Malmuth Marvin (Cal).

GORDY'S DANCER just off the pace away from the rail to the second turn, challenged outside MAGIC MOON leaving that turn, gained the lead in upper stretch and held off MOMS BABY under urging. MOMS BABY between rivals on the first turn, moved up inside on the second turn, angled out into the stretch and finished well but could not catch the winner. CHARISMA saved ground off the pace to the stretch, angled out and just got the show. OH SWEET THING fractious in the gate, hopped at the start, was taken off the rail on the backstretch, raced between rivals on the second turn, angled out for the drive and lacked the needed rally. MAGIC MOON sprinted to the front slightly off the rail into the first turn, set the pace to the stretch and weakened. MADAME BOVARY raced wide throughout. FAGER'S PROSPECT raced off the rail throughout and did not rally. NORTHERN WOOL close up outside the winner to the second turn, gave way and came wide into the stretch.

Owners— 1, Reddam Paul; 2, Johnson & Team Green; 3, Burke Gary W & Timothy R; 4, Potter Gary D; 5, Isabel Stable; 6, Alesia Frank & Sharon; 7, Iron Country Farm Inc; 8, Pegram Michael

Trainers—1, Stein Roger M; 2, Abrams Barry; 3, Mitchell Mike; 4, Fanning Jerry; 5, Perdomo A Pico; 6, Eurton Peter; 7, Lewis Craig A; 8, Baffert Bob

Overweight: Gordy's Dancer (1).

Oh Sweet Thing was claimed by Clear Valley Stables; trainer, Shulman Sanford.,

Madame Bovary was claimed by Blau & Pellman & Schechter; trainer, Cerin Vladimir.

$2 Daily Double (6-6) Paid $64.20; Daily Double Pool $223,706.

THIRD RACE Santa Anita

MARCH 9, 1994

6 FURLONGS. (1.07¹) CLAIMING. Purse $36,000. Fillies and mares, 4-year-olds and upward. Weight, 121 lbs. Non-winners of two races since February 1, allowed 3 lbs. Of a race since February 15, 5 lbs. Claiming price $50,000, if for $45,000, allowed 2 lbs. (Maiden or races when entered for $40,000 or less not considered.)

Value of Race: $36,000 Winner $19,800; second $7,200; third $5,400; fourth $2,700; fifth $900. Mutuel Pool $306,867.00 Exacta Pool $278,216.00 Quinella Pool $43,795.00

Last Raced	Horse	M/Eqt.	A.	Wt	PP	St	¼	½	Str	Fin	Jockey	Cl'g Pr	Odds $1
23Jan94 ^{3}SA^{6}	Miss Inn Zone	LB	6	115	1	1	1^{hd}	1^{1}	$1^{3\frac{1}{2}}$	$1^{3\frac{1}{2}}$	Nakatani C S	45000	1.30
18Feb94 ^{7}SA^{7}	Witch's Power	LBb	4	116	6	5	6	$4^{1\frac{1}{2}}$	4^{3}	2^{nk}	Delahoussaye E	50000	4.10
29Jan94 ^{5}SA^{7}	Wild Express	B	4	116	4	2	3^{2}	$3^{1\frac{1}{2}}$	3^{1}	$3^{1\frac{3}{4}}$	McCarron C J	50000	2.00
5Feb94 ^{7}SA^{6}	Kat Krazy	LBb	4	114	3	3	2^{2}	2^{2}	$2^{\frac{1}{2}}$	$4^{4\frac{1}{2}}$	Gryder A T	45000	10.30
3Aug91 ^{11}SR	Dancing Lindsay	LB	8	114	5	4	$5^{\frac{1}{2}}$	$5^{4\frac{1}{2}}$	5^{8}	5^{14}	Stevens G L	45000	15.70
1Jan94 ^{2}SA^{11}	Palme-Fr	LB	6	116	2	6	4^{hd}	6	6	6	Antley C W	50000	9.70

OFF AT 1:30 Start Good. Won ridden out. Time, $:21^{3}$, $:44^{2}$, $:56^{3}$, $1:09^{3}$ Track fast.

$2 Mutuel Prices:

1–MISS INN ZONE	4.60	3.40	2.20
6–WITCH'S POWER		4.20	2.40
4–WILD EXPRESS			2.20

$2 EXACTA 1–6 PAID $16.40 $2 QUINELLA 1–6 PAID $10.80

Dk. b. or br. m, by Slew's Royalty–Miss Fuddy Duddy, by Fleet Mel. Trainer Spawr Bill. Bred by Jacoby E A & F R (Cal).

MISS INN ZONE dueled inside KAT KRAZY down the backstretch, edged away from that rival leaving the turn and drew clear under steady hand encouragement. WITCH'S POWER moved up three deep leaving the backstretch, found the rail into the stretch and just edged WILD EXPRESS for second. WILD EXPRESS not far back off the rail to the stretch, lacked the needed rally. KAT KRAZY dueled outside the winner for nearly a half mile and steadily weakened. DANCING LINDSAY angled in to race between rivals into the turn and did not rally. PALME off slowly and steadied between rivals at the start, saved ground off the early pace, steadied sharply along the rail early on the turn and gave way.

Owners— 1, Rader & Young; 2, Lanning Curt Or Lila; 3, Lambert Marjorie & Rene J; 4, Lodge Builder Farm; 5, Taub Stephen M; 6, Bollinger Ltd & Ramirez & Varni

Trainers—1, Spawr Bill; 2, Moger Ed Jr; 3, Lukas D Wayne; 4, Ward Wesley A; 5, Hendricks Dan L; 6, Jackson Bruce L

Overweight: Miss Inn Zone (1).

FOURTH RACE Santa Anita

MARCH 9, 1994

6½ FURLONGS. (1.14) MAIDEN CLAIMING. Purse $18,000. Fillies, 3-year-olds, bred in California. Weight, 117 lbs. Claiming price $32,000; if for $28,000, allowed 2 lbs.

Value of Race: $18,000 Winner $9,900; second $3,600; third $2,700; fourth $1,350; fifth $450. Mutuel Pool $302,064.00 Exacta Pool $256,116.00 Quinella Pool $55,481.00

Last Raced	Horse	M/Eqt.	A.	Wt	PP	St	¼	½	Str	Fin	Jockey	Cl'g Pr	Odds $1
	Watching Royalty	LB	3	117	1	11	2^{hd}	1^{1}	$1^{\frac{1}{2}}$	$1^{2\frac{1}{2}}$	Delahoussaye E	32000	3.00
	Tropic Moon	LB	3	117	5	10	6^{hd}	2^{hd}	2^{3}	$2^{\frac{1}{2}}$	Black C A	32000	23.70
23Feb94 ^{4}SA^{2}	Zippen Miss	LBb	3	117	10	3	$5^{\frac{1}{2}}$	$6^{1\frac{1}{2}}$	4^{2}	3^{2}	Stevens G L	32000	3.10
26Feb94 ^{6}SA^{9}	Silent Draw	Bb	3	117	8	1	$3^{2\frac{1}{2}}$	$4^{1\frac{1}{2}}$	3^{hd}	4^{3}	Flores D R	32000	19.20
18Feb94 ^{4}SA^{5}	Lacole	B	3	117	12	4	7^{3}	7^{2}	5^{hd}	5^{hd}	Solis A	32000	5.20
23Feb94 ^{4}SA^{7}	Pocketful Of Bills	LBb	3	115	3	9	11^{hd}	10^{hd}	8^{5}	6^{4}	Nakatani C S	28000	34.20
20Feb94 ^{4}SA^{4}	Drive Thru Daquiri	LB	3	117	7	6	4^{hd}	$5^{\frac{1}{2}}$	7^{2}	$7^{2\frac{1}{2}}$	Antley C W	32000	2.50
24Feb94 ^{4}SA^{8}	Come See Come Saw	LB	3	115	11	2	$10^{1\frac{1}{2}}$	11^{2}	9^{2}	8^{1}	Weinberg A	28000	95.50
	Distant Call	LBb	3	117	4	5	1^{hd}	3^{hd}	6^{hd}	9^{7}	McCarron C J	32000	12.50
	Gamblers Tryst	LB	3	115	6	12	12	12	11^{hd}	10no	Valenzuela F H	28000	33.20
20Feb94 ^{4}SA^{9}	Timealarm	L	3	110	9	7	8^{hd}	8^{4}	$10^{1\frac{1}{2}}$	$11^{1\frac{1}{2}}$	Gonzalez S Jr^{5}	28000	142.70
	New Excitement	Bb	3	110	2	8	$9^{2\frac{1}{2}}$	$9^{\frac{1}{2}}$	12	12	Rojas D S^{5}	28000	129.60

OFF AT 2:01 Start Good For All But DRIVE THRU DAQUIRI. Won driving. Time, $:21^{4}$, $:45^{2}$, $1:11^{1}$, $1:17^{4}$ Track fast.

$2 Mutuel Prices:

1–WATCHING ROYALTY	8.00	5.80	3.60
5–TROPIC MOON		17.20	7.20
10–ZIPPEN MISS			2.60

$2 EXACTA 1–5 PAID $149.40 $2 QUINELLA 1–5 PAID $99.40

Dk. b. or br. f, (Apr), by Slew's Royalty–Lucky Match, by Star de Naskra. Trainer Palma Hector O. Bred by Amory John (Cal).

WATCHING ROYALTY ducked in to be off a bit slowly, was hustled up inside to duel for the lead on the backstrsetch, inched away on the turn, turned back TROPIC MOON in midstretch and pulled clear under urging. TROPIC MOON moved up inside on the turn, angled out to loom a threat outside the winner into the stretch but could not match that rival in the final furlong. ZIPPEN MISS well off the rail on the backstretch, moved up outside DRIVE THRU DAQUIRI on the turn, came four wide into the stretch and finished well. SILENT DRAW forced the early pace three deep, raced four wide on the turn and into the stretch and weakened. LACOLE angled to the rail for the turn, angled out a bit into the stretch but lacked the needed rally. POCKETFUL OF BILLS off the rail early, angled in for the turn, drifted out through the drive and passed tiring rivals. DRIVE THRU DAQUIRI broke in the air and awkwardly, was sent up between rivals down the backstretch but lacked a response in the drive. COME SEE COME SAW raced wide and was outrun. DISTANT CALL dueled between rivals down the backstretch and gave way after a half mile. GAMBLERS TRYST broke slowly, steadied and was outrun. TIMEALARM well off the rail throughout, never menaced. NEW EXCITEMENT steadied when green early and was outrun.

Owners— 1, Amory & Amory & Granja Mexico; 2, Cavanagh Marguerite F & Thomas M; 3, Duray & Jackson; 4, Fields Phillip W; 5, Johnston Betty & E W & Judy; 6, Nowlan Tom; 7, Carondelet Farm; 8, Gordon Jack; 9, Layman George Jr; 10, Bernstein & Jarrell & Spooner; 11, Tam Richard; 12, Stanley Mr & Mrs Robert E

Trainers—1, Palma Hector O; 2, Peterson Douglas R; 3, Jackson Bruce L; 4, Stute Melvin F; 5, Warren Donald; 6, Luby Donn; 7, Hendricks Dan L; 8, Gordon William H; 9, Hofmans David; 10, Raub Bennie H; 11, Lynch Brian A; 12, Neumann Julie

Watching Royalty was claimed by Charles Ronald L; trainer, Shulman Sanford.

Scratched— Natural Value (12Feb94 ^{3}SA^{7})

$3 Triple (6-1-1) Paid $429.30; Triple Pool $119,765.

Furlongs make up a mile in track parlance, and 61/2 furlongs is just over 3/4 of a mile. The standard sprint is 6 furlongs.

The dirt tracks in California are much shallower than those in New York, and therefore the California times are faster. Very few races are run on other than dirt, and unless otherwise mentioned, it is assumed the race was run on dirt. Turf races, of course, are run on grass.

The first race was a claiming race, with a purse of $11,000. Claiming races are the cheapest of all races and generally attract the weaker horses. They're called claiming races because, as we mentioned before, any of the horses running can be claimed by another owner or stable that is racing at that track.

Better horses, or horses with potential, will be run in other than claiming races, for the owners of these quality horses don't want to risk losing their mounts to another owner through a claim. In this first race, the claiming price is quite low, just $10,000. Some claiming prices can go as high as $75,000 and at times even more. Santa Anita is a major track, but in smaller less well known tracks, claiming prices can go down to $1,000.

The low claiming price, and the low purse of $11,000 makes for a field of really cheap horses.

This race is for horses 4 years and older, all at a standard weight of 121 pounds, which is the weight the jockey carries. Non-winners of two races since February 1 are allowed 3 pounds, and non-winners since February 15, are allowed 5 pounds.

Out of a total purse of $11,000, there are distributions to the first five finishers. The winner get $6,050, second $2,200; third $1,650; fourth $825 and fifth $275. With only six horses entered in the race, all but the last finisher is going to get a piece of the purse.

The winner was Diable Rouge, who ran from the number 5 post and was the favorite in the race at 6-5, or $1,20-$1.00. He ran the race in 1.16^2, that is one minute sixteen and two-fifth seconds - two and two-fifth seconds off the track record of 1.14.

Diable Rouge had a five pound weight allowance, and as can be seen, all the horses in the race had weight allowances, all being horses of poor quality, and non-winners for a while.

Diable Rouge wore number 6 and ran from the fifth position probably because of a late scratch. He was second all the way except for the finish where he ran down the leader, Friedlander and won by a neck.

To verify this, we look at the call of the race, just below the Mutuel Prices. *DIABLE ROUGE Jumped a shadow leaving the chute, prompted the pace outside FRIEDLANDER to the stretch and just edged that rival despite jumping the mirror reflection at the wire.*

All the information in the call tells us so much more about the horses than the cold line in the past performance charts. That's why they should be studied by the serious and astute bettors.

Other information about Diable Rouge - his jockey was A L Castanon, and he was by Mamaison (sire) and Crimson Cameo (dam) by Crimson Satan (the dam's sire). The trainer was Sanford Shulman. The owner was Roger J Scarlett. The winner, Diable Rouge, was claimed by David Bowman, and the second place finisher, Friedlander, was claimed by Koriner & Shannon.

There was **Exacta** betting on the race, in which a bettor must pick the exact order of the first two finishers. The $2 Exacta 6-3, paid $15.60. There was also $2 **Quinella** betting, in which the bettor picks the first two finishers in any order to win. This paid $10.20, less than the Exacta, since it's more difficult to pick an Exacta.

There was **daily double** betting as well, in which a player makes one bet to pick the winners of both the first and second races. After the second race, we see that a $2 daily double bet on the winners 6 and 6 (program numbered horses) paid $64.20. Sometimes there's also **Trifecta** betting, in which a bettor must pick the exact order of finish of the first three horses. This paid $2,609.80 for a $2 bet in the fifth race.

At Santa Anita there is usually Quinella and Exacta betting in each race. In addition, there is **Triple Betting** for $3, in which the winners of the third, fourth and fifth races have to be picked. There is also a **Pick Six**, in which the winners of the last six races have to be picked correctly. The most exotic bet is a **Pick Nine**, in which a bettor must select all nine winners to get the big prize.

The charts we've discussed in this chapter give a world of information to the smart bettor. Therefore, you should familiarize yourself with these racing charts, so that you can read them intelligently. This is one of the keys to being a winner at the great sport of horseracing.

VIII. Handicapping A Race

Handicapping, or attempting to pick a winner of a race by an examination of the past performances of the horses in the race, is not an exact science. There are a number of unknown factors, the most important being the condition of the horse on the day of the race. If you're at the track, you can go down to the paddock where the horses are saddled up and look at the horse you want to bet on. But if you're at the OTB office or at a race book, you can't do that.

Even an examination of the horse itself might not tell you much. Thoroughbreds are sleek, powerful animals, bred and built for speed. They are beautiful beasts, but in a race they're all thoroughbreds and all might look good. So, eventually, it's the past performance charts that we must study to find a winner.

The following factors have been suggested by experts and pros at handicapping as important points to note when picking a winner.

1. Study the speed ratings. The horses with the best speed ratings in the race, or second-best, are more consistent winners than horses with lower speed ratings, particularly in sprint races.

2. Look for consistency. Good horses are consistent, and pay particular note to a horse who has been *knocking at the door*, that is, coming in 3rd or second in its last starts. This horse is in shape, and can win.

3. Always give strict attention to a horse that won the last time out, because this horse may be in prime condition and ready to repeat, particularly if it's running in the same class of race against horses it can beat.

4. Pay attention to class. A horse moving up in class is at a big disadvantage, and many false favorites are horses that have won against poorer company and look good on paper, but can't hold their own against better horses.

The easiest way to see this is to study the past performance charts. A horse moving from a claiming to an allowance race is really going in over its head most of the time, as is a horse going from a lower allowance race purse to a higher one. Just examining any past performance charts will show a graveyard of past winners who then finished out of the money when moving up this way.

5. Avoid horses that haven't raced in a long time. They often *need a race* as the handicappers say, to *tighten up*. If a horse hasn't raced in several months, be careful about betting it.

6. Always pay particular attention to beaten favorites the last time out. If they're still being heavily bet, then they are still in top condition. But a beaten favorite last time out who goes off at more than 4-1 is not a good bet. Horses are, for the most part, carefully trained to reach a peak performance, but they generally can't hold that peak for more than a few races, unless they're absolutely top class horses. You must catch the horse during these peak periods to make your score.

7. On off days, when the track is muddy or sloppy, look for horses that break fast out of the gate and can take an early lead. They stand a good chance of going all the way, because the horses behind them will be at a disadvantage with mud in their faces.

8. In fact, it's a good idea to study horses that can break fast and stay first, second or third at the first couple of calls. These horses win more than their share of races.

9. Watch the betting patterns at the track. If a horse is heavily bet down at the last few ticks of the tote board, then "smart money" is coming in. Often this horse, if he didn't figure before on past performance, will run at least third, but might not win the race.

10. If you're at the track, go to the paddock and look at the horses. Avoid those with their ears flat on their heads, or who look frightened, with their heads and eyes lolling about. They're usually bad bets to win the race.

No matter how strong or speedy a horse is, he still must be guided by a competent jockey in order to be a factor in the race. Like all athletes, jockeys run the gamut from the very best to incompetent. A poor jockey can hurt a good horse's chances at winning; a great jockey can help a good horse to win. However, horses that are weak and have no speed cannot be helped by the greatest of jockeys.

Some jockeys, such as Angel Cordero or Willie Shoemaker, have the ability to alter the odds on any horse they ride because of their outstanding skills, and jockeys such as these are such dominant figures that their skills are as important a factor in a big race as is the horse's past performance.

If in doubt, better to go with a *hot* jockey, one who has had a top winning record at the track. This kind of jockey attracts the best horses, and generally has an astute agent who picks winning horses for him.

Above all, find out as much information as you can about the horses you're betting on. And until you feel that you're a good handicapper, bet for fun, and bet the minimum. If you're out at the track, enjoy the day, but don't go overboard and risk too much money. And, of course, if you will be hurt financially or emotionally by betting on horses, don't bet. Only gamble with money you can afford to lose. This is important, don't forget it.

And good luck!!!!

IX. More Winning Tips

Horseracing presents a multitude of variants for the bettor, and this makes picking winners a complex business, even for the experienced and sophisticated bettor. First of all, a field will consist of a number of horses, up to 12 betting choices. Some of these horses will have had recent good races under their belts; others will have had recent poor showings.

Then there is the factor of distance. Some horses will have raced frequently at the distance of the race; others will wither be moving up to the distance and still others will find this a shorter race to contend with. Then there's the track condition, whether it be sloppy, muddy, good or fast. And each track has different soil and different racing conditions.

Often a racegoer will have to handicap a race of 1-1/8 miles in Santa Anita, a fast track, featuring horses that have run in slower times in Arlington Park or Aqueduct. Or some of the horses have done terrifically well at a distance of 6 and 7 furlongs and now are extending their stamina to be tested at the longer distance. A couple of the horses will be moving up in class, and a few moving down in class. The track condition is rated as a "good" for this race.

How can an average racegoer put all these factors into a blender and come up with a winner?

To become a winner at the racetrack, the bettor

must be in a position to handicap each race and select the horse that will win this race. It sounds easier than it is in real life.

There will be many races in which the bettor will face imponderables, in which selecting a winning horse will be like walking through a maze blindfolded. What should the racegoer do in this situation?

He should simply lay off the race and not bet it. The worst thing he can do is throw money away on a race that he or she can't figure out.

Often, ignorant bettors simply look up at the tote board and select the favorite and bet it. Their reasoning is as follows: "I can't figure this race out, but the money is on the 4 horse, and he's a 5-2 favorite. So I"ll simply bet the favorite. He should win, after all he's the favorite."

This is delusional thinking. The bettor thinking this way doesn't realize that thousands of other people at the track have the same thoughts, and thus the ignorant combine with the ignorant to send off a horse as a favorite just because they don't know what else to do.

Favorites win only 34% of the time, and that goes for all favorites at American race tracks. Odds-on favorites, those paying less than even-money to win, will come in for the bettor about 55% of the time. The percentages decrease as the odds go up for favorites.

Thus, you can be sure that even-money choices, going off at 1-1, will win more than 8-5 favorites, who will win more than 5-2 favorites. If favorites of all kinds win only 34% of the time, that means that they'll lose 66% of the time. And 5-2 favorites will be lucky to win much less of the time.

Blindly betting favorites is a sure way to lose money at the track. Not only won't you win, but when you do the payoffs will be small, and you'll miss the opportunity to make big money by betting horses that pay 5-1 or more, where you really start collecting serious money for your wager.

So we come back to handicapping the race, and we must remember that each race presents us with different conditions and different horses, and thus each race must be studied as a separate entity. If you can't properly handicap races, you shouldn't bet money at the track, because the only reason to bet is to win.

Sure, you might say, I'll go to the track and have some fun and wager a few bucks and yell myself hoarse for the horse I've backed. Fine and good. So long as you can afford to lose, and you limit yourself to the few bucks.

But nine races are involved, and often, the bettor who just wants to wager a few bucks, finds himself losing about $30 after several races and now starts to make big bets to try and win it back all at once, and then suddenly finds himself in a big hole, losing money he can't afford to lose. The fun aspect has left. If you don't think this is so, just look at the faces of the people leaving the racetrack after the last race.

No, the fun is in winning, and all the information presented in this book gives you the tools to win.

I would suggest that you first limit yourself to handicapping races at home by purchasing the Racing Form the night before and studying each race and picking a winner. Then go to the track the next day, cut out and eliminate all those horses that have been scratched (removed from the race by their trainers or owners) and watch how the betting goes.

Betting is important, for often there is a clue to where the "smart money" is going. By smart money, we mean money bet heavily by those who have inside information on the race.

Generally, this inside information relates to the condition of a particular racehorse, which the insiders feel can win the race.

They may know this from a variety of factors. They may have seen secret workouts where the horse has shown exceptional speed. Or they may have watched the horse steadily improve, without rushing the horse in previous races, so that his record looks mediocre, but now he's fit for this race and ready to win.

Let's now differentiate smart money from stupid money bet on a horse. The stupid pattern usually is as follows: the track handicapper has made the 7 horse the favorite on the morning line at 5-2. Money is bet on him as the favorite and five minutes before post time, he's 9-5. He goes up to 2-1 and then back down to 9-5, and in the last minute he drops to 8-5.

The vast majority of bettors think that "smart money" has dropped the odds on this horse at the last minute, but what really has happened is that thousands of bettors, unable to determine which horse will win, blindly bet on the favorite at the last minute. Then they watch him lose and tear up their tickets.

Here's how smart money operates. A horse opens in the morning line at 5-1, gets bet down to 4-1 with five minutes to go, then goes down to 7-2 with three minutes to go, and then with each tick on the tote board, drops, to 5-2, 2-1 and then finally goes off at 9-5.

Heavy money is going on this horse and not from the general betting public either. Insiders are betting that this horse can win. He might not win, but you can be sure he has a top chance at winning, and this sort of favorite, or second choice is well worth your bet. Often, it's good to bet this horse across the board, for if he doesn't win, there's a solid chance he'll place or show.

Inside bettors know that this horse is in fine condition. In each race you handicap, you must be sure that your selection is in this fine condition and stands a chance of winning. How will you know? If he has rounded into top shape, finishing fifth, then third, then just missing by a length at second, there is a good chance that he can win this time out. He has been "knocking on the door," as the handicappers say.

A horse that hasn't run for awhile, but has two good races under his belt, running fourth and third, evenly, but has shown good workouts recently, may be due to win. In this case watch the betting patterns closely. If late money comes on this horse, bet him also.

Another thing to look out for is class. Class is represented by the company the horse runs in. If it's a Grade A Stake horse, running in top races like the Kentucky Derby, the horse is of the best class. At the bottom are cheap claimers, running to be claimed for hundreds of dollars. At major race tracks, there will be horses moving up and down in class ever day.

For example, a horse that has run in Allowance races will drop down to a claiming race. Or a horse running as a $15,000 claimer, will move up to a $25,000 claim race. As a general rule, anytime a horse moves down in class, you must give this horse your undivided attention. You may end up not liking him, but you can't just dismiss the horse.

Suppose a horse has moved down in class, unable to compete with better horses, but now is in with cheap claimers. He has finished 8th, 9th and 6th with better company. He is established on the morning line at 8-1, is 6-1 with five minutes to go, and as you look up at the last minute, it goes off at 9-2.

Get some money on this animal. It may not win, but smart money feels it can win, and it may now be in fine condition to do so. You'll have a live animal in the race.

On the other hand, if this same horse, listed at 8-1, goes to 7-1, maybe 6-1, with five minutes to go, but then moves up again to 8-1, and goes off at 10-1, there's no inside money on him. This may not be his day to win. Avoid that horse.

What we're suggesting is to handicap your race the night before, not at the track, so you'll have more time to study the Form, and combine the handicapping with the betting patterns at the track. Both must be taken into consideration.

The thing is, concentrate on each race, then each type of race, and see which you can handicap correctly. If you become a whiz only at distance races of one mile or more, bet them and only them. Don't gamble too much. Don't go to the track to bet on every race. Pick your spots. The most fun anyone can have at the races is to leave with a wallet bulging with cash.

As we showed, there are a multitude of factors. You must eliminate them and concentrate on those factors that you know brings in winners, such as smart money patterns, fine conditions of the horses you bet, horses that outclass the others and so forth.

As you study the Racing Form, your feel for each race will improve. Be patient. Study and handicap, and only when you can win on paper, should you bet. You should be patient at the track and make sure your methods work. Don't just throw money away when you're unsure. And don't bet every race.

It may be difficult to figure out a winning pattern. After all, 95% of horse bettors are losers. But with the knowledge you've gained from this book, and with careful study, you might find a way to consistently win. Then, it will all pay off for you in solid profits.

60

Thoroughbred Horseracing Level II™

Prof. Jones Software - (Available in IBM, Apple, Mac, C/64, TRS)

For players who go to the track once a week or more and desire a **higher winning percentage** and *complete* betting analysis, the Level II is a **very powerful** program with **all the goodies** of Level I plus more. Read on!

Expanded Modules - The **Update Module** compensates for late scratches and holds 50 sets of track, jockeys and trainer records! **Expanded** track configuration uses **Post Bias** for assigning different weights to post positions.

More Features! - The advanced **Fractional Adjusto**r gives accurate early speed and closing abilities of each animal regardless of distance. **Post Bias** is also evaluated for both sprint and route, while the **Master Bettor**™ shows the exact bet, horse and type of bet recommended.

And More Features!! - There's much more to this powerful package - also includes an **on-screen betting philosophy**, a **Horse Watch List**, and a *Pro Series* Money Management strategy! Comes complete with step-by-step instructions, easy-to-read **hardbound manuals**, and **full-service support**! Level II gets beginning and intermediate players winning at the track!

AFTER-PURCHASE SUPPORT - All Prof. Jones software packages have complete 90 day after-purchase support and replacement warranty (and optional 1 year extension) and are backed by 10 years of satisfied customers!

ANALYSIS/OUTPUT MODE
Single key command to analyze race.
Results of analysis shown on screen and/or printed on paper.
Output shown using Charts and Graphs for visual clarity.

UPDATE MODULE
50 sets track records
50 jockey and 50 trainer records
Compensates for late scratches

ENTER MODULE
Single screen input.
All input data can be found on the Racing Form, and is entered in order.